Helping Children See Jesus

ISBN: 978-1-64104-068-6

Christ and the Church
Remember! Repent! Return!
*New Testament Volume 42:
Revelation Part 1*

Author: Ruth B. Greiner
Illustrator: Frances H. Hertzler
Computer Graphic Artist: Ed Olson
Typesetting and Layout: Patricia Pope

© 2018 Bible Visuals International
PO Box 153, Akron, PA 17501-0153
Phone: (717) 859-1131
www.biblevisuals.org

All rights reserved. No part of this publication may be reproduced, stored in a retrieval system or transmitted in any form by any means, electronic, mechanical, photocopy, recording or otherwise, without the prior permission of the publisher, except as provided by USA copyright law.

RELATED ITEMS

To access related items (such as activities, memory verse posters and translated texts) please visit our web store at shop.biblevisuals.org and enter 1042 in the search box on the page.

FREE TEXT DOWNLOAD

To access a FREE printable copy of the teaching text (PDF format) in English or other available languages, enter S1042DL in the search box. Add the item to your cart, and use coupon code XTACSV17 at checkout. Once your order is processed you will receive an email with a link to the free download.

Got Heaven on your mind?

Look at what's ahead!

Revelation 2:10 ♛

Revelation 2:17 Ⓔ

Revelation 2:26, 27

Revelation 3:4-5

Revelation 3:12

Revelation 3:21

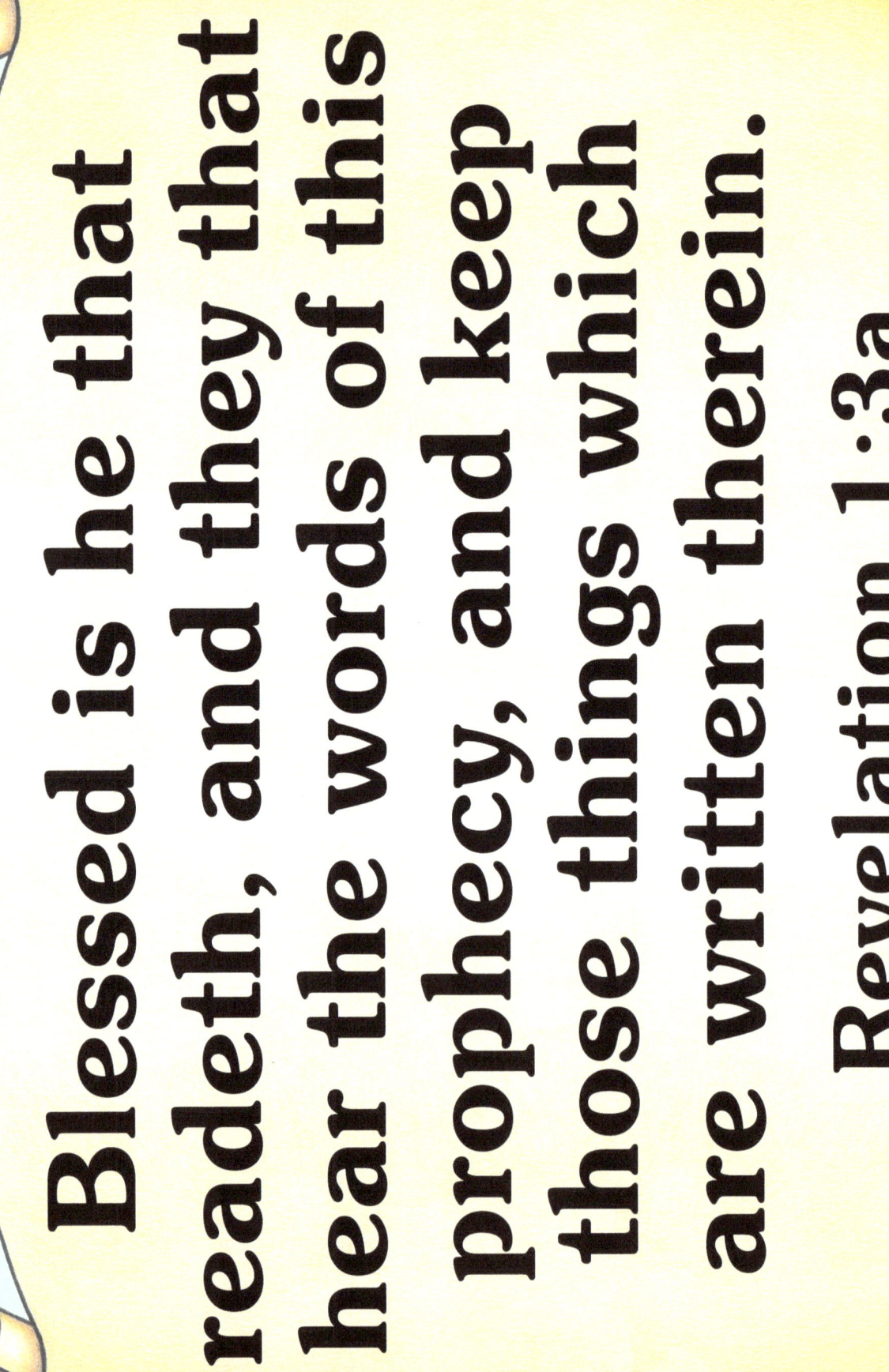

Blessed is he that readeth, and they that hear the words of this prophecy, and keep those things which are written therein. Revelation 1:3a

Lesson 1
THE VISION

NOTE TO THE TEACHER

What blessings lie ahead of you as you teach the marvelous book of Revelation! Each Bible book is important. But the last book is the climax of God's revealed truth. We would not know many of the events of the future if we did not have Revelation.

Although Daniel was commanded *to seal* his book (Daniel 12:40), John was commanded *not* to seal this book (Revelation 22:10). Those who read it are promised special blessing (1:3). So God expects that people who study it will understand it and be helped. Even its title (mentioned in the first verse) indicates that it is a *revelation*–an unveiling–not *hiding*.

It will be of help to you, teacher to memorize the following outline of the book:

1. Description of the risen and exalted Christ (chapter 1)
2. Messages to seven churches in Asia Minor at the time of John (chapters 2 and 3)
3. Description of the throne of God in Heaven (chapters 4 and 5)
4. The coming tribulation on earth with its terrible judgments upon people (chapters 6-18)
5. The second coming of Christ to earth (chapter 19)
6. Christ's reign on the earth for 1,000 years (chapter 20)
7. Description of the new heavens and the new earth (chapters 21 and 22)

There are differences of opinion among those who interpret Revelation. It is the conviction of the publishers of this series that the events from chapter 4 to the end have not yet taken place. They are all in the future. "No judgments in history have ever equaled those described in chapters 6, 8, 9, 16. The resurrections and judgment described in chapter 20 have not yet occurred. There has been no visible return of Christ as portrayed in chapter 19."

Remember! Revelation "is not the only book in the Bible. Let us approach it as worthy of all the Spirit-directed study we can give it, focusing every God-given ability on its words and fitting it into the whole of God's truth as given in the Bible . . . Even though this book is largely about the future, knowledge of it should affect our living in the present. James encouraged his contemporaries with the knowledge of future judgment (James 5:8). Paul wrote of the assurance that Satan would eventually be defeated (Romans 16:20). And God can motivate believers today by the understanding of those things which He has revealed through John in Revelation."

(The above quotations are taken from a volume entitled *Revelation* by Dr. Charles C. Ryrie. It is an excellent volume for all teachers. Available from Moody Press.)

Scripture to be studied: Revelation 1

The *aim* of the lesson: To show that God has a definite plan for the entire future–and He wants to reveal it to all.

What your students should *know*: That the Lord has promised to bless those who read, hear and obey the words written in Revelation.

What your students should *feel*: A desire to understand this prophecy.

What your students should *do*: Study the first two chapters of Revelation every day this week.

Lesson outline (for the teacher's and students' notebooks):

1. The writer–John–on the Isle of Patmos (Revelation 1:1-6, 9).
2. The vision of Jesus Christ (Revelation 1:10-19).
3. Christ and the seven lampstands (Revelation 1:12-13, 20).
4. The coming of Jesus Christ (Revelation 1:7-8).

The verse to be memorized:

Blessed is he that readeth, and they that hear the words of this prophecy, and keep those things which are written therein. (Revelation 1:3a)

THE LESSON

Let us suppose that some dark night, a certain chief calls together the people of his village. In his hand he holds a mysterious-looking object. He whispers, "Under this cover I have a chart listing many things I shall do in the years ahead. I want to show it to you and explain it fully."

Still speaking softly, he adds, "Long ago I prepared a beautiful place for my people. They could have enjoyed it always if they had obeyed me. Instead, they chose to go their own way. So everything was spoiled. Ever since, I have been coaxing them to do as I say. But only a few have loved me and followed my orders. For years, my son and I have been preparing a magnificent new village for these few. However, before we take them to that village, many amazing things will happen. The events are listed on this chart. I am very eager for everyone to know these facts. So much so, that I shall give something special to all who study this chart."

Would the people want to study it? (*Teacher:* Encourage student discussion.) Suppose one says, "I do not care about the future." Or another shakes his head, saying, "I cannot understand charts. I am going home." And both men rise to leave. If you were the chief, what would you say to them? (*Teacher:* Guide students to see that since the future is important to the chief, it should be of importance to his people. In addition, since the chief made the chart, he will help them to understand it.)

In my hand I am holding a copy of God's wonderful Book–the Bible. Actually, it is 66 books, like 66 chapters, all bound together as one book. Each book in the Bible has a name. The first is Genesis. It tells how everything began. The last book is Revelation. It explains how all things will end and where everyone will be forever. Revelation contains so many details it is almost like a chart. God is eager for people to know exactly what is going to happen in the future. So He promises special blessing [happiness] to those who study and obey the teachings of Revelation. (Read Revelation 1:3.) He wants *you* to have this blessing.

1. THE WRITER JOHN ON THE ISLE OF PATMOS
Revelation 1:1-6, 9

Do you know what a "revelation" is? It is the *uncovering* or *unveiling* of certain facts. In the book of Revelation, God, the holy One, has revealed the future. He told the Lord Jesus Christ all that would happen. Christ, in turn, gave the message to an angel. The angel disclosed it to John. And John wrote down everything so we can know what God will do in the days ahead. (See Revelation 1:1-3.)

When the Lord Jesus was on earth, John was one of His disciples. Jesus and John walked and worked together. John saw Christ do many wonders. He saw Him die on the cross for the sins of the whole world. John saw Him after He arose from the dead. He saw Jesus go up into Heaven. That day he heard an angel say, "This same Jesus, who is taken from you into Heaven, will come back in the same way you saw Him go into Heaven." (See Acts 1:11.)

Some years later, John's closest companions (James and Peter) died and went to be with Jesus in Heaven. But John kept busy for the Lord on earth. He preached the Gospel, as Christ had commanded. (See Mark 16:15.)

The Roman Emperor (Domitian), however, did not want people to hear the Gospel. So he punished John by sending him to Patmos Island. Poor John! He was a prisoner on a rocky, lonely, tiny island in the Aegean Sea (between Turkey and Greece).

Show Illustration #1

One day John was thinking seriously about the Word of God. Suddenly something most unusual happened. He could not explain the wonderful feeling he had. It seemed as if he was not in his body any more. Indeed he was in the Spirit. He heard a loud voice sounding like a trumpet behind him. The voice said, "I am the First and the Last. Write in a book what you see. Send the book to these seven churches in Asia: Ephesus [that was where John had been pastor], Smyrna, Pergamos, Thyatira, Sardis, Philadelphia and Laodicea." (See Revelation 1:11.)

2. THE VISION OF JESUS CHRIST
Revelation 1:12-13, 20

John turned to see who was speaking and immediately fell to the ground.

Show Illustration #2

To his amazement, he saw Jesus Christ the Lord! Jesus shone in all His glory–the shining brightness which He had with the Father before the world began. Jesus wore the robe of a priest and judge. (This speaks of His being in authority over His church.) His hair was like snow white wool (a reminder of His wisdom and purity). His eyes flamed like fire (for nothing is hidden from His sight).

His feet glistened like polished bronze. (He is Judge of all the earth.) His powerful voice sounded like a mighty waterfall. In His right hand (the place of honor and authority) He held seven stars. A sharp two-edged sword–the Word of God–came from His mouth. (God's Word judges all people everywhere. See Hebrews 4:12.) Jesus' face shone like the brightness of the midday sun.

No wonder John fell at His feet like a dead man! But Jesus, God the Son, said, "Don't be afraid. I am the first and the last [the eternal One]. I was alive and became dead; and, behold, I am alive for evermore. [I am the Conqueror over death.] I have the keys [the authority] over Hades and death. [I control everything.]" (See Revelation 1:17-18. *Death* speaks of what happens to the *body. Hades* speaks of the realm of *spirits* after they leave the body.)

So John had nothing to fear–not even death. Since he was a true believer in Christ Jesus, death was simply a gateway to Heaven.

John listened carefully as Jesus spoke again: "Write down (1) *the things you have seen,* (2) *the things which are* and (3) *the things which will happen after these things*" (Revelation 1:19).

3. CHRIST AND THE SEVEN LAMPSTANDS
Revelation 1:12-13, 20

John was amazed. The Lord Jesus was standing among seven golden lampstands. In His hands were seven stars. (See Revelation 1:12-13, 20.) What did they mean?

Show Illustration #3

John did not have to ask. Jesus explained, "This is the secret meaning of the seven stars and the seven golden lampstands. The seven stars are the angels [messengers] of the seven churches. The seven lampstands are the seven churches."

John knew and loved these churches and wanted to help them. He was delighted that he–a prisoner–was commanded to write God's message to the churches. Immediately he obeyed and began with a wonderful greeting. "Grace [loving favor] to you and peace from God who is, and who was and who is to come. Grace and peace from the sevenfold [Holy] Spirit. (*Teacher:* Count the statements concerning the Spirit in Isaiah 11:1-2.) Grace from Jesus Christ who faithfully tells the truth. He is the first to be raised from the dead. He is the head over all the kings of the earth. He is the One who loves us and sets us free from our sins by means of His blood. Christ has made us a kingdom of priests to serve God the Father. To Him be glory and dominion forever and ever. Amen." (See Revelation 1:4-6.)

4. THE COMING OF JESUS CHRIST IN THE CLOUDS
Revelation 1:7-8

Show Illustration #4

Then John gave some breath-taking news. "Jesus is going to come back again in clouds. Every eye will see Him . . . The Lord says, 'I am the beginning and the ending of all things. I am the all-powerful One who is, and who was, and who is to come.'." (See Revelation 1:7-8.)

What thrilling news God revealed so long ago! Jesus, who was here on earth (over 2,000 years ago), is coming back. And everyone will see Him. (*Teacher:* This refers to the return of Jesus Christ to the earth *with* His saints, as will be explained in another lesson.)

When will He come to earth? What will happen before He comes? What will believers in Christ do when He comes to earth? What will happen to unbelievers? When will this world end? These questions, and many, many others are answered in the book of Revelation. God has uncovered the future and made it perfectly clear. But–like every Bible book–to understand it, you must study it. Every day, between now and the time we next meet, read Revelation 1:1–2:17. Remember, God promises special happiness to those who read and obey the teachings of Revelation.

Lesson 2
THE SEVEN LETTERS (Part 1)

NOTE TO THE TEACHER

The book of Revelation (according to Revelation 1:19) is divided into three sections:

1. The things which John had seen (the PAST), 1:9-20.
2. The things which are in the process of being fulfilled (the PRESENT), 2:1–3:22.
3. The things which shall be hereafter (the FUTURE), 4:1–22:21.

The first section–the vision John had of the Lord Jesus Christ–was discussed in the preceding lesson. The second section will be taught in this lesson and the next. At the time of John, the seven churches mentioned actually existed in the cities named. Thus it was the PRESENT time.

The seven letters were messages from the Lord Jesus Christ. They were written specifically to those churches. But they are also directed to churches today, since conditions in those churches are similar to those in churches throughout the Christian era. So they have much to say to you, to me, and to those we teach.

Usually these letters follow a pattern:

1. The name of the church to whom the letter is written.
2. A description of the Author, Jesus Christ.
3. The good qualities of the church are mentioned.
4. The serious faults of the church are listed.
5. A remedy is suggested for the problem in the church.
6. A special promise is given to true believers (called "overcomers").

Observe, however, that nothing good is mentioned about two of the churches: Thyatira and Laodicea. No faults are mentioned about two others: Smyrna and Philadelphia.

"The condemnation of the church at Pergamos was in the realm of morals (doctrine of Balaam) and of doctrine (of the Nicolaitans). Balaam (Numbers 22:1–25:9), finding himself unable to curse God's people, instructed Balak, king of Moab, to corrupt them through immorality and idolatry so that God eventually judged them. His doctrine is the teaching of compromise in life. The doctrine of the Nicolaitans may be the same teaching (that is, compromise); or it may be an unwarranted exaltation of the clergy." (Quoted from *Revelation* by C. C. Ryrie.)

Your students may be young or young in the faith. But do not hesitate to teach them from the book of Revelation. Mrs. Gene Ayton (a missionary in Taiwan) writes: "When I was very small, my father read Revelation in our family prayers. I was thrilled and determined to read it for myself as soon as I could. Revelation was the first book of the Bible I ever read all through!"

Symbols (of which there are many in Revelation) delight the young. Your students will experience a real sense of achievement when they discover each symbol's meaning.

Remember, one of the primary rules of teaching is: review, review, review. Using illustrations #1 through #4, allow students to summarize the first lesson. Before beginning this second lesson, let your class members tell what they have learned from reading the first two chapters of Revelation (as assigned in the last session).

We suggest that either before class, or as you teach this lesson, you add the following to the illustrations. (If possible, use one color for the good qualities in each church, another color for the bad traits.) Include the meanings of the names of the cities only if you plan to refer to them when you teach.

Illustration #6
On scroll print *Ephesus* (which means *desirable*). Between two stick men at top right, print this *good* quality: *Rejecting Evil False Teachers*.
Between stick figures in center and those at bottom, print another *good* quality: *Busy for the Lord*.
Under figure of Christ grieving, this *bad* characteristic: *Not Loving the Lord as Before*.

Illustration #7
On scroll print **Smyrna** (which means *bitter*). Starting at bottom left, across page diagonally toward top right, print *Persecution*.

Illustration #8
On scroll print *Pergamos* (which means *marriage*). Top illustration, *bad* characteristic: *Worshiping Religious Officials*.
Bottom illustration, *bad* characteristic: *Allowing Heathen Practices*.

Scripture to be studied: Revelation 2:1-17

The *aim* of the lesson: To impress upon the students that the warnings given to the churches in Revelation are meant also for us today.

What your students should *know*: That God knows everything we do, say, or think–both good and bad.

What your students should *feel*: A desire to obey the whole Word, fearing to disobey.

What your students should *do*:
Unsaved: Place all their trust in Christ Jesus the Lord.
Saved: Confess all sin to God–telling Him exactly what wrongs they are allowing in their lives. Turn from those sins immediately.

Lesson outline (for the teacher's and students' notebooks):

1. John writes the Lord's messages.
2. Letter to the church at Ephesus (Revelation 2:1-7).
3. Letter to the church at Smyrna (Revelation 2:8-11).
4. Letter to the church at Pergamos (Revelation 2:12-17).

The verse to be memorized:

Blessed is he that readeth, and they that hear the words of this prophecy, and keep those things which are written therein. (Revelation 1:3a)

THE LESSON

John was the only Christian on a tiny island. But nothing could separate him from his dearest Friend. Even after the glorious sight of the Lord disappeared (about which we studied in our last lesson), John knew that Jesus was still with him. Christ had promised, "Lo, I am with you always, even unto the end of the world." That promise included the lonely island of Patmos.

1. JOHN WRITES THE LORD'S MESSAGES

Show Illustration #5

John was learning some marvelous truths. The Lord told him to write them in letters to seven churches in Asia. Some letters are very private, they were also written for us today. The instructions in them are for you and for me to read and obey. (See Revelation 1:3.)

In these letters to the churches the Lord had some good things to say. We all like to be told good things about ourselves. The Lord also said some things about the churches which are not too nice. He told the bad things they were doing. Perhaps you and I may be guilty of doing the same wrong things.

Near the beginning of each of the seven letters, Jesus spoke of Himself in a special way. At the end of each letter, He gave a promise to the believers (called "overcomers"–see 1 John 5:4-5). Today we shall look at three of the letters of Christ, recorded by John. (*Teacher:* Refer to the map on the back cover and point to each city as it is mentioned. Also indicate the Isle of Patmos where John wrote the letters.)

2. LETTER TO THE CHURCH AT EPHESUS
Revelation 2:1-7

Show Illustration #6

The first letter is addressed to the church in Ephesus, where John had once been pastor. Ephesus was a famous, large, wealthy capital city in Asia Minor. In the city was the magnificent temple of Diana.

The message to the Ephesian church began this way: "This letter is from the One who holds the seven stars in His right hand. He is the One who walks among the seven gold lampstands." Who is the One who holds the seven stars and walks among the seven lampstands? *(The Lord Jesus Christ)* What do the lampstands represent? *(The seven churches)* The stars are symbols of whom? *(The messengers of the seven churches)*

One of the lampstands represented the church at Ephesus. It is to this church that Jesus was speaking in the letter. He said:

"I know about your works and all that you have done. I know how patient you've been. I know you have refused to listen to evil false teachers. (Point to stick figures at top right.) You have tested those who say they are apostles–but are not. You've learned that they are liars. You have patiently suffered. You have been busy for Me" (Revelation 2:2-3). (Point to illustrations in center and at bottom–people working for the Lord.)

That sounds like a fine church. What could be wrong with church members who make certain that their teachers are true believers in Christ? What is wrong with working busily for the Lord?

The Lord told them: "I have something against you. You do not love Me as you used to. Repent! Turn from your ways. Do as you once did." (See Revelation 2:4-5.)

Jesus added this warning: "If you do not change, I shall come to you quickly [as a Judge]. And your church [lampstand] will disappear."

The Lord loved the Christians in Ephesus. But He was grieved because of their lack of love for Him. (Point to illustration of Christ grieving.) After warning them, He gave them this promise: ". . . Listen to what the Spirit says to all the churches. To the one who truly believes in Me I shall give the right to eat of the Tree of Life which is in the garden of God." (See Revelation 2:7.) What a promise! Someday all true believers will be able to eat of the Tree of Life in the place where God is. There, where there is no sin, they will live with Him forever and ever. What a day!

Sad to say, the church at Ephesus did not listen to Christ's warning. Today that city is in ruins, and there is no Ephesian church.

What about *you*? Are you so busy for the Lord that you are neglecting Him? Have you cooled in your love for Him? If so, He warns you to repent and turn back to Him. Unless you do, He will have to judge you. Remember what He did to the church at Ephesus.

3. LETTER TO THE CHURCH AT SMYRNA
Revelation 2:8-11

Show Illustration #7

The next letter in Revelation is to the church in Smyrna. The word "Smyrna" means *bitter*. In the New Testament it is sometimes translated *myrrh*. (See Matthew 2:11; Mark 15:23; John 19:39.) Myrrh was used in perfume for anointing the dead. It had to be crushed to give out fragrance. What do you suppose happened to the church in Smyrna? Listen carefully!

Smyrna was a wealthy and beautiful port city. It was famous for its Street of Gold. This street led from the temple of Zeus (one of the Greek gods) to the temple of Cybele (the goddess of nature).

The Lord wrote to the church in this pagan city. "These are the words of the One who is the first and the last. The One who was dead and is alive. I know all about your work and your troubles. I know you are poor [in earthly things]. But you are really rich [in God]. I know the evil things said against you by those who say they are Jews but are not. They are on the side of Satan. Do not be afraid of the things that you will suffer. The devil will throw some of you into prison. (*Teacher:* Point to top illustration.) You will be tested and suffer cruelly . . . Be faithful until death and I shall give you a crown of life–an unending glorious future . . . Listen to what the Spirit says to all the churches. Whoever believes in Me will not be hurt by the second death." (See Revelation 2:9-10.) Thus the letter ended.

Jesus knew everything about each church. He knew the bad and good. He knew the past and present. Even more amazing, He knew what was going to happen in the future.

Later, the Christians in Smyrna *were* persecuted. They *did* suffer for their faith just as the Lord had foretold. Some were thrown into prison. Others were doubtless tossed to the lions. (Point to central illustration. Observe, please, that even with the lion's breath on their faces, the couple are trusting God.) Many were lashed. (Point to lower illustration.) Some were put to death.

But Jesus Christ gave two wonderful promises to the suffering Christians. (1) Those who trusted in Him would receive a crown of life. In those days, the winner of a public game (like the Olympics) received a crown of leaves (which would wither). But the Christian's crown of life would last forever. (2) The second promise was that true believers would not be hurt by the second death. They would never be separated from God, regardless of what happened to them on earth. Everlasting punishment would not touch them.

God offered no criticism of the church at Smyrna. It was poor in earthly things. It would suffer persecution. But it was rich in eternal things.

Do you–like the Christians in Smyrna–earnestly witness for the Lord Jesus? Are you willing, should God permit, to die for your faith in Christ?

4. LETTER TO THE CHURCH AT PERGAMOS
Revelation 2:12-17

Show Illustration #8

The third letter is written to the church at Pergamos. From the marketplace in the center of this important city, a person could see a great altar to Zeus. It was built on a hill. Zeus was known as the saviour-god, the chief of the Greek gods. A serpent was used as a symbol of worship. Pergamos was another city of many temples and idol worship. In addition, the people worshiped the emperor.

Satan controlled many of the lives in that city. Some of the people who said they were Christians even married those who worshiped idols. (The name "Pergamos" means *marriage*.)

Listen to what Jesus said to the church in Pergamos. "These are the words from Him who has a sharp sword with two edges–the Word of God. (See Hebrews 4:12.) I know your works. I know where you live–a place where Satan sits. I know you are true to Me. You have not denied your faith in Me, even when Antipas was killed. He spoke for Me faithfully. He was put to death there where Satan is." (See Revelation 2:12-13.)

After these words of praise in Revelation 2:14-15, the Lord said, "But I have a few things against you. Some of your people follow the teaching of Balaam. He taught Balak to set a trap for the Jews. He taught them to do immoral things and to eat food which had been given to idols. (*Teacher:* Point to lower illustration.) Also, you have accepted the false teachings of the Nicolaitans. (*Teacher:* Point to top illustration.) That is, you are giving too much honor to religious officials–almost worshiping them. ["Religious officials" could be *pastors, priests* or *rabbis*.] Some who profess to be Christians are living bad lives." This was exactly what Satan wanted. He wanted to mix false teaching and practice with the Word of God.

"So repent," Jesus said. "Or else I shall come to you [the church] quickly and shall fight against them [those who hold the doctrine of the Nicolaitans] with the sword of My mouth–the Word of God. Listen to what the Spirit says to all the churches. To the person who trusts in Me, I shall give hidden food from Heaven. I shall be sufficient for everything." (See Revelation 2:16-17.)

Then Jesus added another promise: "I shall give a white stone to the one who truly believes in Me. In the stone a new name is written which no one knows except the one who receives it." In those days there was a custom that a judge (when trying a case) would put a white stone and black stone in a vase. When the trial was over, he took out a stone to determine the decision. If he pulled out the white stone, the person was not guilty. If the black stone was drawn out, the person was considered guilty and condemned.

Christ Jesus is saying here that the person who truly trusts in Him is not condemned. He is justified–righteous–and in right standing with God.

Are you a true member of the family of God? If so, have you allowed in your life any of the wrongs that the believers at Ephesus and Pergamos had allowed in their lives? List in your notebook whatever sin you are practicing. Then we shall have a time of silent prayer so you can confess that sin to God. He does not want to send judgment upon you as he did in Ephesus. But He will, if you do not turn from your sin.

Perhaps you have never placed your trust in the Son of God. By refusing to receive the Lord Jesus, you will be separated from God in blackness of darkness forever. Will you turn to the Saviour right now and forsake your sins? God wants you as His own child forever.

ASSIGNMENT: Read the third chapter of Revelation every day until our next session.

(*Teacher:* A principle of God appears in the counsel of Christ to the church at Pergamos. It is this: repent or be judged by the Word of God. This principle has never been changed. It applies to all–both individuals and churches. Unless we are willing to turn from our sins or violations of the Word of God and return in obedience to the Word, we shall be judged by the Word. If we refuse to submit ourselves in this life, we shall face that principle when we stand before the Lord Jesus at His coming. See 1 Corinthians 11:31.)

Lesson 3
THE SEVEN LETTERS (Part 2)

> **NOTE TO THE TEACHER**
>
> In the Revelation of Jesus Christ, He gave seven searching messages–one to each of seven churches of John's day. He commends with absolute kindness. He wars with perfect faithfulness. Do we–like the Lord Jesus–commend our students before mentioning faults? Perhaps we would see greaters results in our ministry if we followed His example. Add the following information to the illustrations.
>
> ## Illustration #9
>
> In the scroll, print *Thyatira* (meaning "never tiring of sacrifice"). Above illustration at top left, print this *bad* characteristic: *Permitting the False Teaching of a Woman.*
> To the right of the idol (top right), print another bad characerisic: *Eating Things Sacrificed to Idols.*
> *Observe that the three figures on the right indicate those who are eating food sacrificed to idols.*
> Above the four singing figures (bottom left), print this good quality: *Increasing in Good Works.*
>
> ## Illustration #10
>
> Print *Sardis* (meaning "escaping ones") in the scroll. At the bottom left, print this *bad* characteristic: *Work Not Complete.*
> *Between the top stick figures, print* Giving to Church Leaders.
> Between the figures on the bottom left, print *Giving to Poor and Sick.*
> Between the two lower illustrations on the right, print *Helping Discouraged.*
> Next to the figure at top right, print this promise: *Faithful Believers Will Reign with Christ.*
>
> ## Illustration #11
>
> In the Scroll, print *Philadelphia* (meaning "brotherly love"). Under the scroll, print this good quality: *Taking the Gospel Everywhere.*
>
> ## Illustration #12
>
> In the scroll, print *Laodicea* (meaning *judgment of the people*).
> At the top left, print this *bad* characteristic: *Believing about Themselves What Is Not True.*
> At the bottom right, print this *bad* characteristic: *Ignoring Christ.*

Scripture to be studied: Revelation 2:18-3:22

The *aim* of the lesson: To show that the Lord is always willing to receive and forgive those who truly turn to Him.

  What your students should *know*: What was true of the seven churches 2,000+ years ago, is true of churches today.

  What your students should *feel*: A desire to earn the rewards promised to believers.

  What your students should *do*:
    Unsaved: Open their hearts and lives to receive the Saviour.
    Saved: Confess and forsake any known sin in their lives.

Lesson outline (for the teacher's and students' notebooks):

1. Letter to church at Thyatira (Revelation 2:18-29).
2. Letter to church at Sardis (Revelation 3:1-6).
3. Letter to church at Philadelphia (Revelation 3:7-13).
4. Letter to church at Laodicea (Revelation 3:14-22).

The verse to be memorized:

Blessed is he that readeth, and they that hear the words of this prophecy, and keep those things which are written therein. (Revelation 1:3a)

THE LESSON

The words of the Lord Jesus are so important, that it is never necessary for Him to say anything more than once. For example, He said, "I am the way, the truth and the life. No one comes to the Father but by Me." (See John 14:6.) Although He never repeated these exact words, there is no other way to come to God except by trusting in Him.

He told one man, "You must be born again." There is no record of His saying this to anyone else. But not a person will ever get into His heavenly home without being born into the family of God.

If things the Lord Jesus said once are of such importance, what would you think about something He said seven times? (*Teacher:* Allow class discussion. Read Revelation 2:7a, 11a, 17a, 29; 3:6, 13, 22.)

Christ Jesus closed each of His letters to the seven churches with this command: "Listen to what the Holy Spirit says to the churches." The warnings He gave long ago are for you and me today. So listen carefully!

John, on Patmos Island, had four more important letters to record for Jesus. He had already finished writing to the churches at Ephesus, Smyrna and Pergamos.

1. THE LETTER TO THE CHURCH AT THYATIRA
Revelation 2:18-29

Show Illustration #9

The fourth letter is addressed to the church at Thyatira. The message began: "These are the words of the Son of God. He has eyes like a flame of fire. His feet are like glowing bronze. (He is the Judge of all.) I know about your works. I know about your love. I know about your patience. The things you are doing for Me now are greater and better than at first." (*Teacher:* Point to illustration, lower left.)

The Lord continued, "But I have something against you. You are allowing Jezebel (who calls herself a prophetess) to teach my servants. She has led them into impurity. And they are eating food that was sacrificed to idols." (See Revelation 2:18-20.)

Jezebel was a wicked woman who lived hundreds of years before this letter was written. She married a king of Israel (Ahab). Until then, the people of Israel had worshiped the true and living God. But Queen Jezebel turned them and their king to worship and serve an idol (Baal). She also taught them to eat meat which had been offered to idols. In addition, she led them into sinful, immoral practices. (See 1 Kings 16:28-33.)

In the church at Thyatira there was a woman whom Jesus likened to the Jezebel of long ago. (Point to illustration at top left.) She taught the Thyatirans to do wrong. She led them in doing immoral things and eating meat which had been offered to idols. (*Teacher:* Point to idol and stick figures on the right.) Actually, she caused them to follow the false teachings of Satan!

In the letter John was writing, Jesus said: "I have given her time to repent and change her mind. But she refused. If you do not repent, I shall punish her and those who have sinned with her . . . I want all the churches to know that I am the One who searches the hearts and thoughts of everyone. I shall reward you all according to your works."

Not everyone, however, was following Jezebel. There were some in the Thyatira Church who did not do evil things. They did not accept Satan's false teachings. To these Jesus said, "Hold on to what you have until I come." (See Revelation 2:24-25.)

Then Jesus gave this marvelous promise to those who truly believe in Him: "If you keep doing My works to the end, I shall give you power over the nations. I shall give you the Bright and Morning Star." (See Revelation 2:26-28.) Think of that! Those who belong to Jesus Christ will reign with Him. And He, the Bright, Morning Star (see Revelation 22:16) promised to be with His own always. He makes it possible for them to shine for Him.

Are you listening to what the Holy Spirit is saying to *you*? Do you worship some false idol–the god of money, perhaps? (*Teacher:* Name any idol that your students may have.) Or is your life pure? Are you shining brightly for the Saviour?

2. THE LETTER TO THE CHURCH AT SARDIS
Revelation 3:1-6

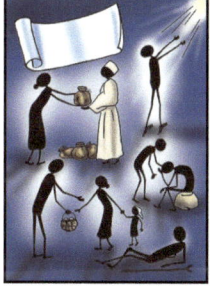

Show Illustration #10

The Lord had a message for another church–the one at Sardis. Sardis was a wealthy capital city built on a hill. To the church there, Jesus spoke of Himself, saying, "These are the words of the One who has the sevenfold Holy Spirit of God (See Isaiah 11:2.) and the seven stars." He has all wisdom and understanding and power. He has control over the messengers of the churches.

Jesus added: "I know your works . . . Others may think you are alive. But you are really dead" (Revelation 3:1). This church doubtless did many good things. They gave money to the church leaders. (Point to stick figures on top left.) They gave to the poor and sick. (Point to stick figures at bottom left.) They helped the discouraged. (Point to crippled person and man on right holding his head.) Many were busy doing nice things. But Jesus warned, "Wake up! Your work is not complete in the sight of God." (See Revelation 3:2.) God expects more of His servants than simply doing good deeds.

". . . Be sorry for your sins," the Lord commanded. "Turn from them. Keep watching for Me! I shall come as unexpectedly as a robber." (See Revelation 3:3.)

Jesus knows everything about every church. So His letter says, "There are a few people in Sardis who are faithful and true to Me. They are worthy to walk with Me. Their names will not be taken out of the Book of Life. I shall speak of them publicly to God the Father and His angels in Heaven." (See Revelation 3:4-5.)

Jesus closed the letter saying, "Listen to what the Spirit says to the churches."

Your name was written in God's Book of Life the day you were born. But your name will be removed from that book if you refuse to believe in the Lord Jesus. And you will be separated from God forever. Christ died so you would not have to receive this awful punishment. If you have never placed your trust in Him, will you do so right now?

3. THE LETTER TO THE CHURCH AT PHILADELPHIA
Revelation 3:7-13

Show Illustration #11

The sixth letter was written to the church in Philadelphia. Philadelphia was important because one of the main roads for trade and postal service ran through the city. Armies and merchants traveled this road. There were great possibilities of reaching people *from* and *in* other cities. It was an open door of opportunity.

To the church at Philadelphia Jesus said, "These are the words from the One who is holy and true." The Lord Jesus Christ cannot sin for He is holy. He cannot lie for He is truth. Everything He does and says is right.

He added, "I am the One who opens and no one can shut. When I shut, no one can open." How can this be? Because He has all authority, all power. (See Matthew 28:18-20.) It is impossible for anyone on earth to close the doors of Gospel preaching unless the Lord allows it. For He is in control of everything!

"I know your works," the Lord told the Philadelphians. "Because there are so few believers, you are not very strong. But you have obeyed My Word. You have not denied My name." (See Revelation 3:8.) The people were taking the Gospel everywhere. (Point to illustration.)

Christ Jesus gave some wonderful promises to His own in Philadelphia. "I shall *keep you from* the time of trouble which will test everyone in the world. We will learn about this dreadful time of trouble in a later lesson.) I shall come quickly . . . I shall make each true believer a pillar in the temple of God." (See Revelation 3:10-12.) In those days pillars were sometimes marked with the name of a person who was being honored. What a privilege to be honored of God in His eternal temple! "And," the Lord promised, "I shall write the name of My God on My own." He wants all to know that He belongs to them and they belong to Him.

The letter ends with, "Hear what the Spirit says to all the churches."

Have you been listening? Are you–like the faithful believers in Philadelphia–sharing the Gospel with others? Will the Lord be able to reward you for your witness?

4. THE LETTER TO THE CHURCH AT LAODICEA
Revelation 3:14-22

Show Illustration #12

The last of the seven letters is addressed to the church at Laodicea. At one time it was one of the wealthiest cities in the world. Jesus said, "These are the words from the One who is faithful, the

One who tells what is true, the One who made everything in God's world." (See Revelation 3:14.)

He continued, "I know your works. You are not cold nor hot. I wish you were cold or hot. Instead, you are only slightly warm. So I shall spit [vomit] you out of My mouth." (See Revelation 3:15-16.)

Cold water is a great help to a person who is hot and thirsty. A hot drink is satisfying to one who is cold and shivering. But slightly warm water neither refreshes nor satisfies. Indeed, it can make a person sick! The people of the church in Laodicea were only slightly warm toward the Lord. And this was sickening to Him.

So He told them, "You say, 'I am rich and do not need anything.' You do not know that actually you are pitiful, miserable, poor, blind and unclothed." (See Revelation 3:17.) They were believing about themselves things which were not true. (*Teacher:* Point to left-hand illustration.)

Christ urged the Laodiceans, "Come to Me for true riches, purity, spiritual sight." (See Revelation 3:18.)

He could not praise them for anything. But He did remind them of His love. "Those whom I love," He said, "I speak to with strong words. And I punish them. Oh, please do what I say. Be sorry for your sins. Turn from them. Listen! I am standing at the door, knocking. (*Teacher:* Point to illustration on right.)

If anyone hears My voice and opens the door, I shall come in to him. I shall eat with him and he with Me." When anyone receives the Saviour, the Lord takes whatever that person offers Him. But He *gives* that person all His riches. Imagine that!

To those who truly believe in Him, He promises, "I shall allow you to sit with Me on My throne." (See Revelation 3:19-21.)

This letter (like the other six), closes with, "Listen to what the Spirit is saying to all the churches."

Have you really listened to what God said to the seven churches? If the Lord Jesus spoke to you right now, would He praise you? Or would He condemn you? Have you truly trusted in the Lord Jesus Christ? Or is He outside of your heart and life? He loves you with all His heart. He is waiting to give you everything you will need for this life and the life after death. But He will never force you to place your trust in Him. If you believe He is God the Son who died and rose again, will you *receive Him this moment?*

(*Teacher:* Urge each one to list his sinful practices in his notebook. Lead students to confess these sins. Have them write down exactly how they plan to turn from these sins this week.)

ASSIGNMENT: Read the first three chapters of Revelation daily.

Lesson 4
THE CHURCH

NOTE TO THE TEACHER

In the Old Testament Tabernacle, the only light came from the golden lampstand. Each of its seven branches had a little lamp. The lamps were set in such a way that they gave light "over *against* the lampstand." (See Numbers 8:1-4.) There was a blaze of light on the central shaft of the lampstand. It was caused by the united shining of the lamps.

This is a beautiful Old Testament illustration of a New Testament truth. When the Lord Jesus was on earth, He said, "You are the light of the world . . . Let your light so shine before men, that they may see your good works, and glorify your Father which is in Heaven" (Matthew 5:14, 16). Those of us who have placed our trust in Christ are to shine for Him by our good works. Everything we do is to show up the glory of the Lord–not our own glory. If our teaching impresses the class only with the abilities of the teacher, the lamp has failed. It has shined over against itself instead of over against Him.

Certain members in the seven churches mentioned in Revelation were pleasing God by the way they shone. Others were not shining. What about you, teacher? Do your pupils constantly see the love and light of Christ Jesus reflected in your life? May it be so.

Turn Illustration #13 sideways. Beneath the long, thick line, add the information which follows. This may be done while you are teaching, or beforehand. During the early part of the lesson point to *each illustration* as it is mentioned.

Starting at left, under the appropriate illustrations, print:

ADAM and EVE	Birth of CHRIST	The Coming of the HOLY SPIRIT
The TABERNACLE	Death of CHRIST	CHRIST the HEAD of the CHURCH
	Resurrection of CHRIST	

Scripture to be studied: Revelation 1:1–3:22

The *aim* of the lesson: To show that God has planned everything from beginning to end.

What your students should *know*: God has revealed His plan so all may know it.

What your students should *feel*: A desire to turn from everything that displeases Christ the Lord.

What your students should *do*:
Unsaved: Open their hearts and lives to the Saviour.
Saved: Examine their lives carefully, determining to live so as to receive the rewards Christ has promised His own.

Lesson outline (for the teacher's and students' notebooks):

1. The plan for the Church (Matthew 16:18; 1 Corinthians 12:12-13; Ephesians 1:22-23; Colossians 1:18).
2. The Head of the Church is Judge of all (John 5:22, 27).
3. The good and evil in the Church (Revelation 2:2-20; 3:4-17).
4. The rewards for the Church (Revelation 2:7, 10, 17).
5. The Lord's invitation (Revelation 3:20).

The verse to be memorized:

Blessed is he that readeth, and they that hear the words of this prophecy, and keep those things which are written therein. (Revelation 1:3a)

THE LESSON

Genesis, the first book in the Bible, is the book of beginnings. Revelation, the last book, is the book of last things. As we read the Bible from Genesis through Revelation, we learn that God has always had a marvelous plan. And that plan includes you and me.

1. THE PLAN FOR THE CHURCH
Matthew 16:18; 1 Corinthians 12:12-13;
Ephesians 1:22-23; Colossians 1:18

Show Illustration #13

In the very first book of the Bible, we are told that God visited certain people here on earth. (Point to illustration on left.) He walked in the Garden of Eden and talked with Adam and Eve. (See Genesis 3:8.) Later God was among His people in the Tabernacle. (See Exodus 40:34-35.) Even though they could not see Him, they were assured of His presence with them.

Many years later, God did something even more wonderful. He Himself, in the person of His own dear Son, came to earth. The people could see Him. They could talk to Him, touch Him, listen to Him speak. But Christ died. For three lonely days His followers were separated from Him. Then He arose from the grave! Once again He was with them. Forty days later He went up into Heaven. No longer could the people on earth see Him or touch Him.

But God always wants to be with His people. So, according to His plan (see John 14:16-17), He sent His Holy Spirit to earth (on Pentecost). People could not *see* His Spirit. How could they be certain He had come? God announced His coming this way: He caused an echoing sound as of a violent wind. He sent tongues of fire which divided and settled upon the heads of Christ's followers. God gave them the ability to tell His wonderful works in languages that were foreign to them but known to the listeners. (See Acts 2:1-4.) All who were gathered that day learned that the Spirit of God had come. From then on, His Spirit has lived within those who belong to Him. (See 1 Corinthians 6:19; 2 Corinthians 6:16; compare Ephesians 1:13; 4:30.) And they belong to His Church. (Sometimes the Church is called the Body of Christ. See 1 Corinthians 12:12-13.)

However, there was one who was not at all happy with the plan of God. He is the enemy of the Church. His name is Satan. Ever since the beginning, Satan has fought against God. He does not want anyone to serve the Lord. The Church is made up of those who have turned from Satan, choosing to serve God. For that reason, Satan hates the Church.

It is God's plan to build His Church. (See Matthew 16:18. Remember, this Church refers to all *people* who belong to Christ. It does *not* mean a church *building*.) People from all parts of the world make up His Church. Each becomes a member when he chooses to trust in the Lord Jesus Christ. This is the only way a person can become a member of the Church, the Body of Christ.

As a physical body must have a head, so the Body of Christ must have a Head. God has named the Lord Jesus Christ as the Head of the Church. (See Ephesians 1:22-23; Colossians 1:18.) Everyone who belongs to Him is to worship and serve Him. (*Teacher:* Point to far right of illustration #13.)

According to the plan of God, believers in Christ living near each other, worship Him together. These groups became known as churches. In time, some of these groups built buildings which were also called churches. It is sad that many became members of these churches without belonging to the true Church–the Body of Christ. They were never born again into the family of God.

In our first three lessons from Revelation, we have been learning about seven churches in Asia. Do you remember their names? *(Ephesus, Smyrna, Pergamos, Thyatira, Sardis, Philadelphia, Laodicea.)*

2. THE HEAD OF THE CHURCH IS JUDGE OF ALL
John 5:22, 27

When John had his vision on Patmos Island, did he see the actual churches? (*Teacher:* Encourage student participation throughout the balance of the lesson. They should, if possible, read these truths from the Bible and enter them in their notebooks. Use appropriate illustrations from this volume.)

No, John did not see the churches. (Read Revelation 1:12, 20b.) He saw seven lampstands. (Show Illustration #3.) Did he see a messenger from each of the seven churches? (Read Revelation 1:16a, 20a.) Who held the seven stars in His hand? (Revelation 2:1). Who had the sharp sword with two edges? (Revelation 1:16; 2:12). What is that two-edged sword? (Ephesians 6:17b; Hebrews 4:12).

The Lord Jesus Christ, in shining, bright glory in Heaven, was also revealed to John. He looked like a man of authority wearing the long robe of a priest and judge (Revelation 1:13). His hair was a reminder of His wisdom and purity. Why? (Revelation 1:14a). His eyes saw everything. What did they look like? (Revelation 1:14b). With such eyes, He sees what is in each person's heart and mind. He knows everything. And He controls everything.

For those who have received Him as Saviour, these are marvelous truths. To others, this is a frightening revelation.

Show Illustration #14

The Lord Jesus, in Heaven with God the Father, is all knowing. As Judge, Jesus will one day punish all who have not placed their trust in Him. Their names will not be written in the Book of Life unless they trust in the Saviour in this life. If not, they will be separated from God forever. (See Revelation 20:11-15.)

3. THE GOOD AND EVIL IN THE CHURCH
Revelation 2:2-20; 3:4-17

Today, the Lord Jesus sees you. He sees me. He sees us inside and out. What does He see?

As with the churches in Asia, He sees the good things His people do. He sees those who refuse to listen to evil false teachers. He sees the people who are busy working for Him (as in Ephesus). (Show Illustration #6.)

He knows when His own are persecuted. He sees all who keep right on trusting God (as with the Smyrnans). (Show Illustration #7.)

He knows those who stay true to Him (as in Pergamos), even when others do not stay true to Him. (*Teacher:* Show Illustration #8).

He knows the people who are serving Him more acceptably than they used to. There were some like this in Thyatira. (*Teacher:* Show Illustration #9).

He sees those who are faithful to Him as were the few in Sardis. (*Teacher:* Show Illustration #10.)

He is pleased to see those who take the Gospel message to others, as did the Philadelphians. (*Teacher:* Show Illustration #11.)

Show Illustration #15

The Lord Jesus knows each one who has turned to Him. (*Teacher:* Point to left side of illustration.) They know He is the Son of God. (See 1 John 4:15.) They admit they are sinners (Romans 3:23; 6:23). They believe Christ died for them. (See Romans 5:8; 1 Corinthians 15:3-4; 1 Peter 2:24; 3:18.) And they place all their trust in Him, receiving assurance of eternal life. (See John 3:16-18; 6:37.)

Have *you* turned to the Lord Jesus? Or have you turned away from Him? (*Teacher:* Point to right side of illustration.) If you refuse to receive Him, you will be separated from God forever.

Because the Lord sees all and knows all, He also detects evil as He did in the churches long ago.

He is grieved by those who do not love Him as they once did. He keeps an eye on those who are busy, but neglecting Him, as in Ephesus. (*Teacher:* Show Illustration #6.)

He is sad when people follow heathen practices and mix false teaching with the Word of God, as they did in Pergamos. (*Teacher:* Show Illustration #8.)

He knows those who listen to the teaching of evil men and women. (Show Illustration #9, Thyatira.)

He knows those whose work for God is not complete. (*Teacher:* Show Illustration #10.)

It is sickening to Him to see people working halfheartedly for Him. They are "lukewarm," like the Laodiceans. (*Teacher:* Show Illustration #12.) He is brokenhearted when people neglect Him, even locking Him out of their lives.

What did the Lord Jesus say to the people in the churches who were doing evil? He commanded, "Remember . . . Repent . . . Return." And that is exactly what He says to you today, if you are doing evil. *"Remember* how far you have fallen. *Repent,* change your ways. *Return* to Me and serve Me in the right way." If your life has not been pleasing to Him, will you confess the wrongs to Him right now? (See Proverbs 28:13.)

4. THE REWARDS FOR THE CHURCH
Revelation 2:7, 10, 17

Today, as in the long ago, the Lord Jesus has rewards (in this life and the next) for those who truly trust in Him and have hearts fixed toward Him. If you are one of these, you will live forever in the garden of God. (See Revelation 2:7.)

Show Illustration #16

Each one who is faithful to Christ, even through testings, will receive from Him a crown. (See Revelation 2:10; James 1:12.) As we shall see later, the crowns He gives His own will be their gifts to Him (Revelation 4:10-11).

He promises to provide His children with everything they need in this life. (See Revelation 2:17; Philippians 4:19.)

He declares they are righteous–in right standing with God. They receive a "white stone." (See Revelation 2:17.)

Those who truly trust in Him will reign with Him. (See Revelation 2:26-27.)

The Lord Jesus Himself, the Bright and Morning Star, will always be with His own–now and forevermore. He will speak of them publicly to God the Father and His angels in Heaven. (See Revelation 3:4-5.)

God will honor the true believer in His eternal temple. He will write His own name on each one. (See Revelation 3:12.)

All who belong to Christ Jesus will sit with Him on His throne. (See Revelation 3:21.)

It is hard to imagine that God has such tremendous rewards. But it is true, for it is part of God's perfect plan. He wants *you* to have these rewards.

Jesus Christ, God the Son, is looking into your heart and life right now. Does He see good? Or does He see evil?

5. THE LORD'S INVITATION TO ALL
Revelation 3:20

Show Illustration #17

If you have never trusted in Him, He is standing at the door of your heart. He is knocking and waiting. He wants to come in, but will never force you to receive Him. He waits for you to open the door. Will you do so–right now?

www.ingramcontent.com/pod-product-compliance
Lightning Source LLC
Chambersburg PA
CBHW060800090426
42736CB00002B/99